Let Your Voice Be Heard

Don't Suffer in Silence

Sam Granger

Illustration by: Katelyn Crouch

Charleston, SC
www.PalmettoPublishing.com

Let Your Voice Be Heard

First Edition

Printed in the United States

ISBN-13: 978-1-64990-433-1
ISBN-10: 1-64990-433-9
eBook ISBN: 978-1-64111-231-4

Table of Contents

(Scared To Love You)

There's something I wanna say
But every time my heart beats the wrong way
My mind races
I see the past
That fire burning seems to last
Tired of being hurt
So destroyed from work
Between my mind and my hand
I'm not sure you understand
Understand all the abuse I have took
From my work, my bio dad, hello my own brother
Brother lied so I got beat by my mother
Feelings are dangerous for me
It opens doors
Doors of the past and for the present
I say it in my mind
But I freeze in person every time
So scared of being hurt
Always fearing I will lose all that I have
I know your different
Not like the rest
I'm hoping my fears fade away
The end I say
Til yet another day
As alwayz
-Samantha May-

(Surprised)

Surprised your ok with looking into my eyes
My eyes that show all my pain
Pain, scars, and a damaged soul
Soul that's broken but far from weak
Weak is something I will never be
Be true to myself that's how I live
live is such a powerful thing to say
Say what's on your mind
Mind how the past has changed us all
All good things eventually come to end
End this day with no regrets
Regrets only eat you alive
Til your dead
The end I say
Til yet another day
As Alwayz-
-Samantha May -

(Truth)

Do what you do
Say what you say
Don't live another day
Another day without people knowing who you really are
Another day without simply being yourself
I'm odd I'm strange
Maybe even a little deranged
I have done my share
I have done my part
I've made a difference in this world
We can live
We can dream
Life is not as hard as it may seem
Every day the sun will rise
Every day the sun will set
It's up to us to live without regret
The end I say
Til yet another day
As Alwayz
-Samantha May-

(Life As It Is)

6 years ago today
Not a tattoo on me
Less scars then to show
On 1.21.12 at 4:59 am
I brought a life into this world
I felt alone I felt brave
I knew to work I'd be a slave
For my ex is nowhere to be seen
A single mom I knew I would be
Stephan has everything he needs
Thanks to me and my family
My family for raising him strong
For being there when I'm at work so long
Today a happy birthday boy he will be
For were all home thankfully
The end I say
Til yet another day
As alwayz
-Samantha May -

(Succubus)

Looking like you care
Don't you dare
You can't fool me
I look into your eyes
I can see your lies
One day your judgement will come
They say the truth will set you free
But you'll never confess to all that you've sinned
The pain you've caused
The lives you've hurt within
One day you'll end up in the ground
But you were never around
Never around to be missed
Never around to be heard
The end I say
Til yet another day
As alwayz
-Samantha May-

(Last days)

My heart stopped
As the world turned still
I was prepared for the worst
Drs said she was very ill
Days went by
No hope in sight
She started to breathe
She started to fight
I call everyday
I never want it to be her last
I'm sorry if my pain is pushing people away
I can't stop caring
I won't stop sharing
Somethings just need to be said
Next tattoo won't be for me if I lose you
The end I say
Til yet another day
As alwayz
-Samantha May -

(Words aren't just words to me)

People say
I'd die for you
I'd lie for you
I'd take a bullet for you
But would they really?
I know I would
I'd take someone else's pain
I'd do whatever I could do
For I could not live with myself knowing
Knowing I could have done more
I hate saying goodbye
I hate knowing the end may come
That's a reality I may soon face
So bare with me
My mind is a mess
My nerves are shot
I'm just hoping for a good ending plot
The end I say
Til yet another day
As alwayz
-Samantha May -

(Ptsd)

It's like you went to war
But you didn't come back
I turned around and said where you at
It's like a bad car ride
And you just wanna hop out
It's like being on a plane
And being told you can't land
Like I'm stuck on replay
And can't get the record to spin
The cd keeps skipping
Playing that beat over and over again
Reminding me of the pain I feel with in
Never did I wanna say goodbye
Never did I see it happening this way
The end I say
Til yet another day
As alwayz
-Samantha May -

(Mono Days)

In bed
Am I alive
Am I dead
Or is this a bad dream
Why does this happen to me
Try and save the world
It backfires
I come down with the plague
Can't walk or move a leg
Every breathe feels like my last
Don't know what's worse
It's like a curse
My past forever haunts me
A cold became asthma
My life forever changed
Being helpless drives me insane
All I can do is weep and pray
That I will get better one day
The end I say
Til yet another day
As alwayz
- Samantha May-

(Choices)

Don't be a trigger
I've already been put through the ringer
Never again will I bow down
Bow down from what I believe
Bow down to your level and deceive
Mouthy I can be
Crazy the good kind I perceive
I live a life like no other
I know of no soul that can walk in my shoes
At the end of your day it's what you chose
You chose how to react
You chose to not care that's a fact
I live every day to make a difference
I live to try and change this cruel shallow world
The end I say
Til yet another day
As alwayz
-Samantha May -

(Defect)

The pain in my spine
Is making me blind
Dizzy to my core
Simple tasks take so long
The symptoms I chose to ignore
Not much can help me
For I was born this way
No pain or no sleep
Is the fight I have inside my head
Some days it's easier to just lay awake in bed
Tomorrow I will persevere
For another 15-hour day awaits me
The end I say
Til yet another day
As alwayz
-Samantha May -

(On Repeat)

One day I won't wake up alone
One day I won't stare at my phone
One day my happiness will be real
One day I will truly be able to feel
To feel normal inside to feel safe and not hide
To call a place home to not be afraid to be alone
Alone with these thoughts in my head
Always afraid to go to bed
For every time I close my eyes
He's there haunting me like a bad scene out of a movie
But there's no power off for it
It replays inside my mind
Time heals most wounds
All but the ones you have to talk about to let go
The end I say
Til yet another day
As alwayz
-Samantha May -

(A. M. K)

I never wanted to fall
For some reason he stayed through it all
I tried my hardest to push him away
Yet he pushed me right back everyday
He refused to let me go
He chose to see if my heart would bleed red again
I didn't want to care
This life hasn't been fair I didn't want to put my heart out on the line
One morning I awoke I knew I wanted to be by his side
I said I'd never love again I was only looking for a friend
A friend to get me through my dark times
A friend who listen and not judge my mind
Fate has its way of showing us what we need
The end I say
Til yet another day
As alwayz
-Samantha May-

(Disappointed)

Now he's dead
What can be said
Burying your brother you should of known
You saw the pain in your mother's eyes
Yet your own life you despised
Were all left to mourn your loss
I'm sorry your demons got the best of you
Your kids still have their mother
Your left with one last brother
I hope you watch over them all
I hope your there when they shed a tear
I hope your with Michael in heaven
The end I say
Til yet another day
As alwayz
-Samantha May-

(Sealed Fate)

I'd say heaven gained an angel
But I'd be lying
You're definitely a devil without wings
All the pain you caused me and others
Then you just go and end it all
Must be nice was the famous line you'd say
I'm sad for I have to explain you to a child you barley knew
Because you were so eager to be with your friends Funny how their all dead now just like you
Mixed emotions panic attacks hit me through out the day
The good memories of you keep flooding my brain
I'm trying my best to stay sane
Your looking down on me and can now see our child learn and grow
Your stupid to end your life this way
As you already know because I've already yelled it and cried about it
Knowing you'd see the grief you've caused
I need all the strength I can get
To survive these next of hard days
The end I say
Til yet another day
As alwayz
-Samantha May-

(Some Days)

Some days I can go a week without you
Sometimes I can't go a day
Some days I wanna lay in bed forever
Sometimes I wanna explore
Some days I never wanna leave
Sometimes I feel it's too good to be true
Some days I can't sleep
Those days I ask to stay with you
Those days I may not sleep but I feel less alone
Those days will hopefully get better once this process comes an end
I don't know what imma do with you
I hope to never live a day without you
The end I say
Til yet another day
As alwayz
-Samantha May-

(R. M. W.)

Say what you will
The man that hurt me
Showed me what love was
That man that threw me
Watched me get back up 10 times stronger
That man that stalked me
Taught me always watch my back
That man that called me 100 times
Showed me he was determined to hear my voice
That man that broke me
Showed me the signs of abuse
That man that left me
Regretted it every day
That man wasn't the man I met
The man I met showed me how to fish
The man I met loved racing and fixing cars
The man I met was by my side when I was sick and ready to die
The man I met saved me inside
The man I met gave me happiness
The man I met I knew I'd always love
The man I met was my everything
The end I say
Til yet another day
As alwayz
-Samantha May -

(I Knew)

I knew once I told you there was no going back
Would you pass all my test
Or would you walk away and just laugh
So here we are months later in time
I never thought you'd be mine
For I never thought this would work
Yet somehow it does
You have yet to complain
I stopped waiting for that day
You're not the type to truly yell
Or blame me for everything
I've learned you're not out to change me
Which is kind of a relief as well
I like my wicked ways and this is who I am
Laying next to you
I feel comfort looking in your eyes
I don't fear you're out to get me
And ruin me with lies
Oh how the people in my past I despise
I'm living for today
I'm not worried about a future
For everything happens for a reason
Every stone has a place
Every heart has a beat
Every shadow disappears in the sun
Every morning I wake up I roll over and kiss you
The end I say
Til yet another day
As alwayz
-Samantha May-

(If I Could)

If I could lay in bed with you every night I would
If I could silence all your thoughts I would
If for just a day I could take away all your pain I would
If I could show you my world through my eyes I would
Then maybe you'd understand
Understand that I'm not going to hurt you
Understand that your way isn't always best
Understand that change can be good
Understand that everyday there's something to be learned
The end I say
Til yet another day
As alwayz
-Samantha May-

(You've)

You've given me a comfort like no other
You were there for me when my brother betrayed my mother
You didn't know it
But you we're always just there
Hidden in the background
Without a sound
It will be sad when you're not around
I always came to you to protect me
Or for guidance
For I know you weren't the kind to judge
You need to move on
Move on from a company that doesn't let you grown
Doesn't appreciate you and boy does it show
Were all unhappy
Tired of pulling the burden of certain others
Those that hide under the covers
Don't be the mattress beneath the sheet
So to speak
You'll be ok
Your stronger than you know
True friends follow you wherever you go
The end I say
Til yet another day
As alwayz
-Samantha May -

(Escapade Over)

Moved away
Had nothing to say
What we had was just a game
It's such a shame
Wish the good times didn't end
You come into my store
You look at me like a sore
As if the wound is still fresh
My feelings weren't hurt
For I had no feelings at all
You were a fun time
I never wanted you to be mine
A hello here and there
I miss the cuffs on the bed
Is all that needs to be said
The end I say
Til yet another day
As alwayz
- Samantha May -

(Hopes)

You've never heard me sing
I wanna learn to dance
I want you to see true romance
Marry me
Carry me
Carry me up the stairs like in the movies
Throw me into the bed
Climb on top of me and rest your head
Rest your head knowing you've found the one
The one who will take care of you
The one who can't leave too many dishes in the sink
The one who's as stubborn as you
The one who inspires you to think
To think of your goals and your dreams
To remind you what happiness is all about
The end I say
Til yet another day
As alwayz
-Samantha May -

(Hate)

I hate that your miles away
I hate that you feel quiet today
I hate that you can't hold me in your arms
I know
I know that one day I will meet you
I know that I'm glad you came along
I know my time will come
I believe
I believe that everything happens for a reason
I believe that we will have happiness one day
I believe surviving the worst has prepared us for the best
I love
I love that you make me laugh
I love that you accept me for who I am
I love that your brave enough to put me I'm my place
The end I say
Til yet another day
As alwayz
-Samantha May-

(Ended Love)

I'm afraid to love
Yet I don't wanna the feeling go
I'm afraid to care
But your making me dream of there
I'm scared that this will all end
Somehow be pretend
Just a game per say
I like hearing you
I like seeing you
I hate that I'm so attached
At times I wanna walk away from it all
Fearing I'm gonna fall
That no one will be there once I hit the ground
I won't make a sound
Simply suffer in vain
I know you not like the rest
My mind likes me to suffer
Thoughts sit on buffer
Like a bad movie stuck on replay
Thoughts stew all day
They say you'll back out
That this isn't meant to be
That it's too much to be with me
Sad but true
It's not easy telling myself I will one day have you

(One Day)

One day I roll over and you'll be next to me
One day you won't be a phone call away
One day you'll be mine forever
Someday
Someday you'll know what an equal relationship is
Someday we will travel the world together
Someday we will climb a mountain and just sit and embrace
Soon
Soon you'll look in my eyes and know how I feel
Soon you'll throw me in bed and lose the key
Soon we will playhouse and know this was meant to be
The end I say
Til another day
As alwayz
-Samantha May-

(Misogynist Manager)

Can't let it go
So here we go
That's a low blow
I didn't come for you to put on a show
The audience stood still
You tried to put on a thrill
I told you no
You insisted anyway
Wish cameras had sound
Wish you didn't get away with pushing me around
Say what you will
But a liar I will never be
I don't know why you had to cause a scene
Belittle me
God don't like ugly
He's bound to show you that your wrong
Family for life
Don't make me start carrying a knife
Next time you'll regret challenging me
One on one
I know I will win that fight
I don't need a crowd saying my name
Your face in the ground
Or your back walking out that door
Pick your poison just stop targeting me
Never did I lie
Why would I waste my time
Your fears will be the death of you
The end I say
Til yet another day
As alwayz
-Samantha May -

(Long Distance Lover)

I feel
I heal
I dream of you
I wish
I hope
That I get to meet you
I like your voice
I like your face
You make my heart race
I need
I want
To be close to you
You make me happy
You make me smile
This is too good to be true
When I feel this way
It's like something could ruin it all
I never get to be happy
Something always ruins it
But it's always people on drugs
Which I know you wouldn't touch
Yet my mind fears I'm gonna lose you
And that would put me in a dark place
I need to hear you're not gonna up and leave
That it's just my mind playing games
Driving me insane
Can't wait to hop on a plane
And see you face to face
Hold you, touch you
Make your heart run in place
The end I say
Til yet another day
As alwayz
-Samantha May-

(Fallen)

I think I'm falling in love
I think it's a sign from up above
Not all are created equal
Finally someone that has proved my past wrong
Someone that listens
Someone that nods and agrees
When he sees I need to vent
This anger I've carried for so long
Finally, can be set free
All because he truly cares
And doesn't want anything from me
He doesn't want my money
He doesn't mind my ink
He just wants my time
To help clear my mind
And maybe a smile or wink
To show that I care
That I have an ounce of hope within
Maybe I can start over
And my dream can be real with you
The end I say
Til yet another day
As alwayz
-Samantha May -

(Love Never Dies)

Could of been a family
Could of been married
Could of been dead
I just wanna be happy in my head
Why did drugs have ruin it all
I was ready to catch him if he had to fall
I watched him stop breathing
I watched him suffer
I watched it consume him
All that's left are the ashes of what would of been
Could of been
Will never be
The end I say
Til yet another day
As alwayz
-Samantha May -

(M.E.C)

I remember when we made amends
I remember when we were able to be friends
I remember all the emotions I felt
I remember you calling for him
I was home alone
I answered the phone
I remember asking you for the truth
I remember all the questions in my head
I remember talking to you for hours
Lying in a dark room in bed
I remember talking to you everyday
I remember the pain going away
I wish you didn't leave for that party
You knew I had nowhere to go
He told me you never called
That you were with someone else
I remember you coming back the next day
I remember not knowing what to do or say
I have a few regrets
But I know you knew how I felt
I remember you getting home
I remember the hopes and dreams you had
I wish I had called you that night
I wish you could of been saved
I fear you may of made the same decision though
The end I say
Til yet another day
As alwayz
-Samantha May-

(You)

You used to feel like mine
Now you're just floating in space with nothing to hold on to
Not sure what happened
It's like a breaker blew
That I'm still waiting for the lights to come on
Life overwhelms me
All I wanted was you
My cries for help went unanswered
Before I knew it I was on the ground
When I awoke I couldn't hear a sound
I've been sick all my life
In pain that slowly grew to more
Rots me to my core
Every breath I take feels like my last
Everyday I'm alone I think of my haunting past
The demons set in
One day they may not leave
I'm okay with that
For I've accomplished a lot in this world
The end I say
Til yet another day
As alwayz
- Samantha May-

(Ghoster)

She fed him lies
Id soon despise
Every day it's like reliving the past
Everyday I'm reminded of the wounds deeper than the last
He says he'd never hurt me
Never have a forcing hand
I know these words are because of her
It's been months of hearing this
It's getting to me
His walls are still up
I wish he'd just trust me
I'd do anything for him
I'd take all his pain away if I could
I see her name
It drives me insane
I remember going through hell and back
The sleepless nights
The quiet days
That puppy dog look for days
The pain that forever haunts him
The pain that's holding him back
Sorry isn't good enough for what you've done
That's not a lie it's a solid fact
The end I say
Til get another day
As alwayz
-Samantha May-

(Dark to light)

I brought light to your darkness
I tried to heal your soul
Some wounds were too big to close
The gap couldn't dispose
I let you into my world
Showed you how different life can be
I only wish you'd listen to me
Things could be better
Life can change as quick as the weather
Like sunny to dark
Like a fire that has a spark
My love for you will continue to grow
I'm your ride or die as you know
Never thought you'd me mine
Never planned this in time
All these years you've been my friend
All these years you played pretend
You pretended to be set in your ways
You pretended to live in a haze
Deep down your willing to change
Deep down we are both strange
Salute to many adventures to come
Salute to the steps we may take
Salute to making each other better in ways
Salute to your love I crave
The end I say
Til yet another day
As alwayz
-Samantha May-

(Katie)

My sister Katie
Such a lady
She can draw
Not a flaw
If only you saw
How great you are to me
When you were born
The world stood still
Knowing you were ill
But we wouldn't know that for months to come
A fighter you became
For all the battles you would face
No one could ever take your place
Years passed by
You grew strong
No weakness in sight
You can accomplish anything
Just follow that passion
And you just might
Might have your art on a book cover
At work people think I'm your mother (lol)
You want to help the world
Your heart shines so bright
Follow your dreams
Life isn't always a fight
If Ever a doubt
Just know that I'm there
Only phone call away
I'd do anything for you
Can't wait for you to graduate hurray

The end I say
Til yet another day
As alwayz
-Samantha May-

About the author.

Sam Granger is from Brooklyn Park Maryland. Her family moved to the Eastern Shore when she was 4 to give her a better life. Sam is an aspiring writer and health care worker. When she was three, she knew her dream was to heal the world. She went to school to be a nurse. She is currently a Direct Support Professional to help Autistic Individuals meet their goals to be a functioning adult. She previously worked for a department store but realized she wasn't appreciated and deserve the respect she had earned. Sam is currently going to college to further her dreams in the health care field. Sam has had a lot of support along the way. Her support system includes her parents Thomas & Bonnie, her son Stephan and her two sisters Jackie& Katie. Sam's goal with this book is to inspire others to speak up and to be their true self.

www.ingramcontent.com/pod-product-compliance
Ingram Content Group UK Ltd.
Pitfield, Milton Keynes, MK11 3LW, UK
UKHW051206260726
13967UKWH00011B/3127